HONEY BEES

Drawings by Klarie Phipps

COVER PHOTO: Donald Specker/Animals Animals

Page 5 M.A. Chappell/Animals Animals; page 7 Grant Heilman/Grant Heilman Photography; page 9 Grant Heilman Photography; page 11 Grant Heilman Photography; page 15 Carson Baldwin Jr./Animals Animals; page 17 Treat Davidson/National Audubon Society/Photo Researchers; page 19 M.A. Chappell/Animals Animals; page 21 Oxford Scientific Films/Animals Animals; page 23 Harry Rogers/Photo Researchers; page 25 David Thompson-Oxford Scientific Films/Animals Animals; page 27 Oxford Scientific Films/Animals Animals; page 29 Scott Camazine/Photo Researchers; page 31 Irwin L. Oakes/Photo Researchers.

Library of Congress number: 89-3909

Library of Congress Cataloging in Publication Data

Kahkonen, Sharon.
  Honey bees/Sharon Kahkonen.

  (Real readers)
  Summary: Identifies the different types of bees within a honeybee hive and describes their physical characteristics and their functions.
  1. Honeybee — Juvenile literature. [1. Honeybee. 2. Bees.] I. Title. II. Series.
QL568.A6K34 1989   595.79'9 — dc20   89-3909
ISBN: 0-8172-3508-6

1 2 3 4 5 6 7 8 9 0   93 92 91 90 89

Honey Bees

by **Sharon Kahkonen**

Raintree Publishers
Milwaukee

BUZZ BUZZ! Look at all the **honey bees**!
The bees are busy in the **beehive**.

All the busy bees have jobs to do.

A beehive has 1 **queen bee**. She is the biggest bee. She lays all the eggs.

This is what the queen bee looks like.

Queen Bee

A beehive has **drone** bees. A drone's job is to mate with the queen.

This is what a drone looks like.

Drone Bee

There are lots of **worker bees** in the beehive. The worker bees have lots to do. They have to go out and look for food.

This is what worker bees look like.

Worker Bee

A worker bee that finds food goes back to the beehive. The bee **dances** to "say" where the food is. The **round dance** means the food is near the beehive. The **wagging dance** means the food is not near the beehive.

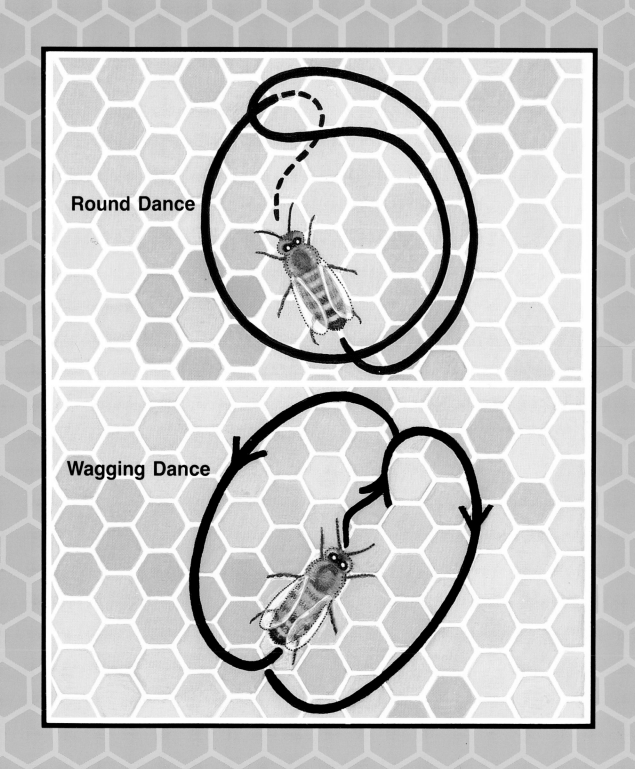

Round Dance

Wagging Dance

The worker bees find food in **flowers**. They sip **nectar** out of flowers. They pick up little bits of **pollen**, too. Nectar and pollen are food for the bees.

There are little bags on the worker bee's legs. The bee can fill the little bags with pollen. Then the bee can take lots of pollen back to the beehive.

When a worker bee has lots of pollen and nectar, it goes back to the beehive. There, all the bees will eat nectar and pollen.

The worker bees take the nectar and pollen and make things for the beehive, too. The worker bees make honey out of the nectar and pollen. They make **wax** out of the nectar and pollen, too.

Pollen Bag

What is the wax for? The bees press and poke the wax to make little wax cups. All the little cups have 6 sides.

The bees fill lots of cups with honey. They put wax caps on top of the filled cups. When the bees need food they eat the honey in the cups.

The workers make wax cups for the queen bee, too. She lays eggs in the wax cups. A queen bee can lay 2,000 eggs in a day!

Now the eggs are in the little wax cups. In 3 days, little grubs come out of the eggs.

The worker bees feed the little grubs. The grubs eat nectar and pollen. They eat honey, too. The grubs eat and eat. They get bigger and bigger.

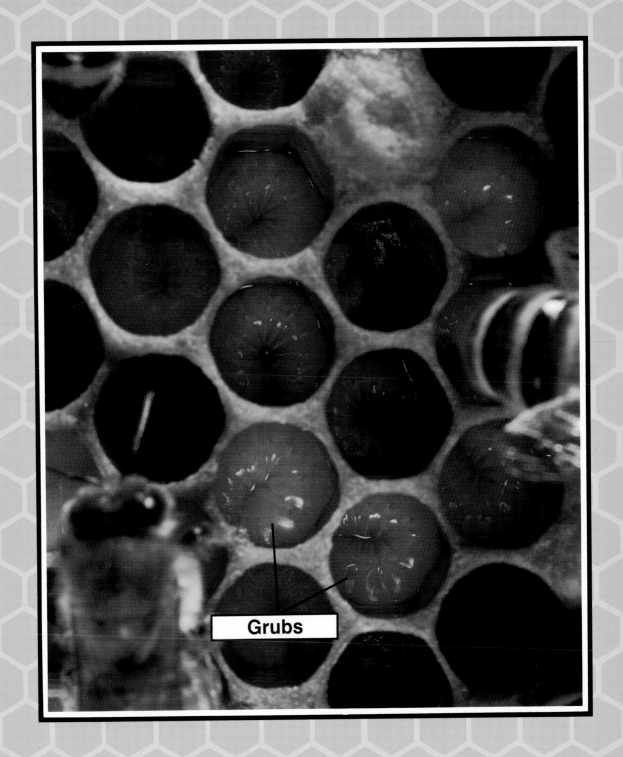

Grubs

Now 2 more days have passed. The grubs are big. The grubs stop eating, and the worker bees put wax caps on the little wax cups.

Wax Caps

Now 8 more days have passed. The grubs are bees now. They poke out of the wax cups. They will have jobs to do in the beehive.

If there is a lot of food in the beehive, the queen bee lays more and more eggs. In time, there are more and more new bees. The beehive gets bigger and bigger.

If a beehive gets too big, 1 grub will grow to be a new queen bee. Now there are 2 queen bees. The new queen bee will keep the beehive.

The old queen bee goes out of the beehive. Lots of bees go with the old queen bee. They will make a new beehive.

The bees get busy and make the new beehive. The worker bees make little wax cups. A drone bee mates with the queen bee. The queen bee lays eggs in the cups. In time, new bees come out of the little wax cups.

The beehive gets bigger and bigger. The bees have lots to do. BUZZ BUZZ! You can see the bees keeping busy!

Sharing the Joy of Reading

Beginning readers enjoy reading books on their own. Reading a book is a worthwhile activity in and of itself for a young reader. However, a child's reading can be even more rewarding if it is shared. This sharing can enhance your child's appreciation—both of the book and of his or her own abilities.

Now that your child has read **Honey Bees**, you can help extend your child's reading experience by encouraging him or her to:

• Retell the story or key concepts presented in this story in his or her own words. The retelling can be oral or written.

• Create a picture of a favorite character, event, or concept from this book.

• Express his or her own ideas and feelings about the subject of this book and other things he or she might want to know about this subject.

Here is an activity that you can do together to help extend your child's appreciation of this book: Discuss that honey is an enjoyable food for people. You and your child can make this snack using honey. You will need: 1 firm banana, $\frac{1}{2}$ cup honey, $\frac{1}{2}$ cup wheat germ or crushed cereal flakes (e.g., cornflakes), 1 plastic knife, toothpicks, 2 small bowls, and a plate. Peel the banana and cut it into bite-sized pieces with the plastic knife. Place a toothpick in each piece of banana. Dip each piece of banana into the honey, then into the wheat germ or cereal. Place the pieces on the plate. Then eat!